Cumbria
County Council
Libraries, books and more . . .

Please return/renew this item by the last due date.
Library items may be renewed by phone on
030 33 33 1234 (24 hours) or via our website
www.cumbria.gov.uk/libraries

Cumbria Libraries
CLIC
Interactive Catalogue

Ask for a CLIC password

Lots of things
you want to know about
ASTRONAUTS
...and some
you don't!

Written and
illustrated by
David West

W
FRANKLIN WATTS
LONDON•SYDNEY

First published in the UK in 2014 by Franklin Watts

Franklin Watts
338 Euston Road
London NW1 3BH

Franklin Watts
Level 17/207 Kent Street
Sydney, NSW 2000

Dewey classification: 629.4'5

A CIP catalogue record for this book is available from the British Library.

ISBN: 978 1 4451 2719 4

Franklin Watts is a division of Hachette Children's Books, an Hachette UK company.
www.hachette.co.uk

LOTS OF THINGS YOU WANT TO KNOW ABOUT ASTRONAUTS ...AND SOME YOU DON'T!
David West Children's Books, 6 Princeton Court, 55 Felsham Road, London SW15 1AZ

Designed and illustrated by David West

Printed in China

Contents

The first astronaut was a dog

People began building spacecraft in the 1940s. Before people were sent into space, scientists needed to know how spaceflight would affect living things. So spacecraft were launched into space using animals.

In 1957 the first animal to **orbit** the planet was a stray dog from the streets of Moscow. Her name was Laika, which means 'barker' in Russian.

The first person in space was a cosmonaut

In 1961 a **Soviet** pilot, named Yuri Gagarin, made the first journey into outer space. He made a complete orbit of the Earth in Vostok 1 before landing safely back on Earth. Soviet spacemen are cosmonauts, which means 'universe sailor' in Russian.

Early spacecraft had room for only one astronaut

A month after Yuri Gagarin's epic flight, Alan Shepard became the first American in space in the 'Freedom 7' capsule. The spacecraft was so tiny that people said the astronaut wore it like clothes.

Giant rockets fire spaceships into space

To escape the earth's **gravity**, large rockets are needed to blast astronauts into space. The largest were the Saturn V rockets. They were 110.6 metres tall and weighed 2,800 metric tons. That's about the same as 450 elephants!

Russian spacecraft land with a bump

Spacecraft use parachutes to slow them down before landing back on Earth. Russian Soyuz capsules fire rockets seconds before landing to soften their touchdown on the hard earth of Kazakhstan.

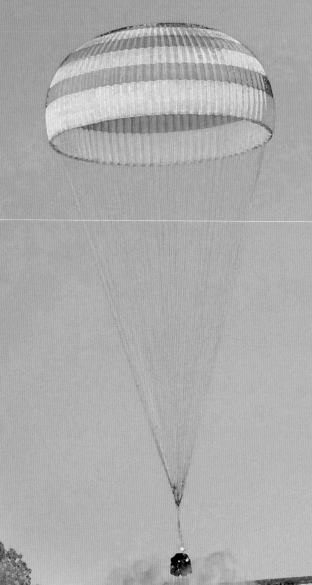

American spacecraft landed with a splash

Before the Space Shuttle was built, returning American space capsules landed in the ocean. After splashdown the spacecraft, with its astronauts still inside, was picked up by a helicopter, which took it to an **aircraft carrier**. Later, crew were released from the capsule before it was airlifted back to a ship.

An eagle landed on the Moon

Launched by a Saturn V rocket on July 16, 1969, the spacecraft, Apollo 11, headed for the Moon. On July 20 the **Lunar Module**, called the 'Eagle', was the first manned mission to land on the Moon. Six hours after landing Neil Armstrong stepped onto the Moon.

You can jump higher on the Moon

Astronauts who visited the Moon discovered that they had to move in shuffling bunny hops. This is because the Moon's gravity is weaker than Earth's. Astronauts can jump about six times higher on the Moon than they can on Earth!

Astronauts went for a drive on the Moon

When Apollo 15 astronauts touched down on the Moon, they had an extra-special tool packed away on their lunar module. It was a lunar rover that enabled them to become the first people ever to drive on the surface of the Moon.

Apollo 13 missed the Moon

56 hours into their trip to the Moon, the astronauts of Apollo 13 heard a loud bang, followed by **thrusters** firing to correct the spaceship's position. An oxygen bottle had exploded in the **Service Module**. The crew had to abandon the Moon landing and use the Lunar Module as a lifeboat. They travelled around the Moon before returning safely back to Earth.

The Space Shuttle was a reusable spacecraft

The Space Shuttle was used on 135 missions from 1981 to 2011, all launched from the Kennedy Space Center in Florida, USA. The Shuttle consisted of a spaceplane for orbit and re-entry, fuelled by an external fuel tank, with reusable, strap-on, solid booster rockets.

The boosters returned to Earth by parachute and the spaceplane glided back after re-entering Earth's atmosphere. The external fuel tank burnt up in the atmosphere after it was **jettisoned**.

Five spaceplanes, Columbia, Challenger, Discovery, Atlantis and Endeavour were built. Two, Challenger and Columbia, were destroyed in accidents and their entire crews were lost.

Astronauts put a **telescope** in space

The Space Shuttle's many major missions included launching numerous satellites and **probes** to the planets, conducting science experiments, and building and servicing the International Space Station.

The Hubble Space Telescope was carried into orbit in 1990 and still operates today.

Space suits are like mini spaceships

Outer space has no air and can be very hot or cold. A space suit keeps astronauts safe, supplying them with oxygen, temperature control, a communication system, and waste management (a toilet system). There is even a strap-on rocket pack which allows the astronaut to move about just like a spacecraft.

People live in space

Circling the Earth in outer space is a space station where astronauts work for months at a time. It is called the International Space Station (ISS). It orbits Earth between 330 and 435 kilometres away and completes 15.7 orbits each day. Electrical power is supplied by large **solar arrays**.

Tourists visit the ISS

Astronauts and supplies are ferried to and from the space station by Soyuz spacecraft. Sometimes seats are available and sold to 'space tourists' for about £24 million each.

Astronauts' taste buds don't work as well in space

Scientists try to make food especially tasty on the ISS because people's sense of taste is reduced in space. The **galley** has two food warmers, a refrigerator and a water dispenser for heated and unheated water.

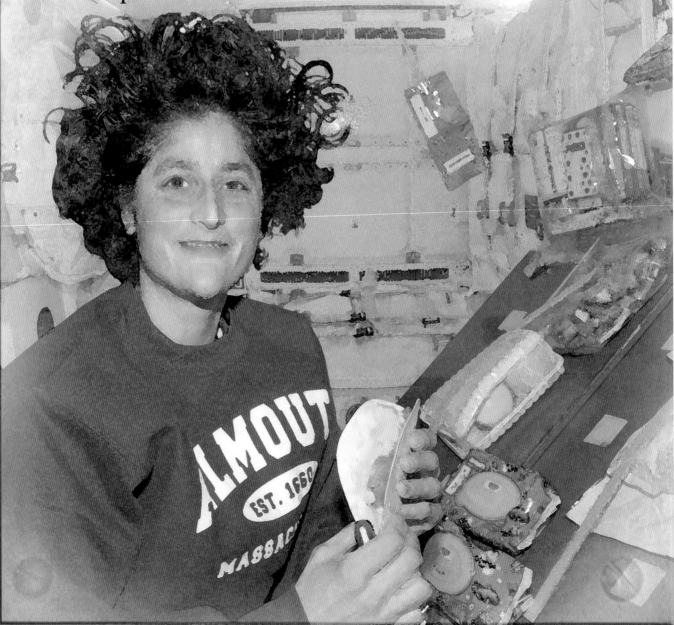

Astronauts can sleep upside down in space

Because there is no gravity, there is no right way up in space. Astronauts can sleep in any direction. They are zipped into a sleeping bag that is attached to a wall so they don't float away. Sleeping in space is very easy and relaxing.

One day astronauts may visit planet Mars

Although many probes have successfully landed on Mars, humans have not made the trip. A trip to Mars and back would take 400 to 450 days, which is much longer than a year. In 2012 a private project named 'Mars One' was announced. It aims to establish a settlement on Mars in 2023!

Glossary

aircraft carrier A ship with a large deck, which aircraft can use.

galley The part of the space station where food is prepared and cooked.

gravity The invisible force of an object that pulls other objects towards it. The larger the object the bigger the pull. The Earth's gravity keeps us from floating away.

jettison To drop or get rid of something.

Lunar Module The lander portion of the Apollo spacecraft that landed on the Moon.

orbit In this case, the path of an object around a planet.

probe An unmanned spacecraft.

Service Module The part of a spacecraft attached to the Command Module. It supplies electrical power and storage for oxygen.

solar array Panels of cells that convert sunlight into electricity.

Soviet The name for anything Russian between 1922 and 1991.

telescope An instrument that magnifies objects in the distance so that they appear nearer.

thrusters Small rocket engines.

Index

A

Apollo 10, 12, 13
Armstrong, Neil 10

C

cosmonaut 5

F

Freedom 7 6

G

Gagarin, Yuri 5, 6

H

Hubble Space Telescope 16

I

International Space Station (ISS) 16, 18, 19, 20

L

Laika 4
lunar lander 12
Lunar Module 10, 13
lunar rover 12

M

Mars 22
Mercury 6
Moon 10, 11, 12, 13

P

probe 16, 22

S

satellite 16
Saturn V 7, 10
Service Module 13
Shepard, Alan 6
Soyuz 8, 19
Space Shuttle 9, 14, 16
space suit 17

V

Vostok 1 5